Tomorrow's World Order Answering the Critics &
Debunking the Misconceptions.

DEDICATION

A better new world.

Tomorrow's World Order
Answering the Critics & Debunking the Misconceptions

Overall, "Tomorrow's World Order" proposes a drastic overhaul of the current global order but faces significant challenges with regards to scientific soundness, democratic considerations, and practical implementation. While it prompts discussion about pressing global issues and potential solutions, careful analysis and critical thinking are crucial in evaluating its feasibility and potential consequences.

"Tomorrow's World Order presents a bold and thought-provoking vision for the future. While it raises concerns and complexities, it also highlights the need for innovative solutions to address pressing global problems."

David Gomadza

The First Global President of the World

www.twofuture.world

ISBN: 9798875726903

TABLE OF CONTENTS

According to him he was killed by his stepfather the day he got a new second

ACKNOWLEDGMENTS

To Tomorrow's World Order.

QUICK SUMMARY

Tomorrow's World Order. The Constitution: & Our Important Principles" by David Gomadza, the organization aims to introduce

1. A new system of governance that emphasizes the printing of new money as the only true source of growth and individual, national, and global wealth.
2. They also aim to introduce a global leader who represents all mankind and leads all nations acting as an overseer and guiding force with the aim of taking humanity out of the defensive stages where weapons and defense take center stage.
3. They also aim to ban global wars, weapons manufacturing, possession, and trading, as well as killings of innocent women and children globally.
4. They aim to shift the thinking from austerity: living within your means, to an emphasis on growth giving the people more power in decisions and policies that affect them

CONTROVERSIAL PARTY IDEOLOGIES AND CRITICISM OF TOMORROW'S WORLD ORDER'S IDEOLOGIES. CONCERNS WE MUST ADDRESS.

These are the potential concerns about Tomorrow's World Order:

- *Loss of sovereignty: The idea of a single global leader raises concerns about loss of national sovereignty and potential for abuse of power.*

We are not going to replace country leaders and their government with ours. I must stress that we are not to take over as such. We are just going to sit on top of everyone and let the people do what they do best, especially regarding country specific issues. Instead, we are going to have the last say when it comes to global problems like poverty, effects of climatic change, unemployment, high inflation, and all economic and financial crises. We are only putting a central decision-making body for things that affect the world as a whole. We will not change a thing, especially the first years. In the first year our aim is to increase cooperation, trust building, mediate and facilitate and even help your leaders regardless of how they have been in the past. We are to augment the system by providing a quick solution to central issues.

The loss of sovereignty is incorrect because we are not changing countries or their leaders, we are just taking over critical decision making on things that are global like climate change and poverty. One of our guiding principles as per our constitution is recognizing individual country's sovereignty. No country will lose its sovereignty because of Tomorrow's World Order.

We are to leave the countries as they are for a year or two even after then what we will do is to nominate our own leaders who will democratically challenge their leaders through the ballot. That means when fully operational we will put leaders from the same country as leaders of that country without changing anything.

All these leaders will be answerable to me [David Gomadza] as I am the first global president of the world. That means we are just putting a post that is higher than the current system without many changes at the lower level. But I make decisions and set targets, for example like the global minimum wage for the whole world. Which is currently at US$17 this year 2024.

My job therefore becomes that of setting global targets and standards. I will now, after setting the standards, require every country on earth to work harder and do whatever it takes so that by the end of 2024 at least the minimum wage in this country will be as close to the global minimum wage of US$17. I can also impose sanctions or punishment for countries that do not meet these global minimum standards and fine them until they have pegged the minimum wage close to this global standard.

I can also introduce a weapons manufacturing levy on top of country specific levels that penalizes the manufacture and use of weapons that are used in conflict zones and where there is proof that the weapons were used to kill women and children. I will fine both the manufacturing company and the country concerned as well as individuals who might have negligently contributed to the deaths of women and children.

We can actually strengthen national sovereignty by providing a judicial review that is listened to and abided by everyone. I can use our laws to ban invasion of a sovereign country. We will have the power of asking for soldiers from each country for peace's sake. We can ask for 10 000 soldiers from each country on earth to defend an invaded country and maintain security and peace. All current institutions like the UN cannot do this.

We can override decisions of powerful regimes, cults like NATO, Soviet Pack, etc and function as mediators and conflict resolution entities meaning protecting a country's sovereignty.

Addressing concerns of the potential abuse of power.

We represent the entire world. I and three others will become overseers, mediators, peacekeepers, defenders of the innocent and defenseless in women and children and conflict revolutionists and mediators. We are not becoming dictators but act like guardians who are entrusted with global funds and trust for preemptive action to fight effects of natural disasters caused by climatic change and effects of wars.

HOW ARE WE GOING TO BE JUST AND RUN THE WORLD AS JUST RULERS?

I have decoded the brain, DNA sequencing, dreams, God or Yahweh, the tree of life, brain reading and all brain codes. This means that I can read the brain just like the creator does. I can just sit down and look at someone's eyes and know everything that person did.

The brain uses Yahweh's time 23:90 that means one hour of Yahweh's time has 90 minutes. This means you must add exactly 30 minutes to normal time to know what the brain has recorded. Likewise, if reading brain thoughts, you must subtract 30 minutes from the time to know exactly what time it was, for example when an accident happened.

I can read the brain thoughts of up to ten people at the same time, something that has never been done before. This is the first time you have heard this. That means we will be just, and we can present exactly as it happened and the people's thoughts.

No one can lie to use. This is because we can include brain thoughts linked to nerve impulses at that time to know exactly what a person was thinking at a given time and place.

Only Yahweh or God can do this.

WHY CAN WE DO SOMETHING ONLY THE CREATOR CAN DO?

I have decoded God, that is Yahweh, enough to have his DNA sequence so that I am able to look at someone, a picture, a video and know exactly what he did and what his brain thoughts, action potentials and nerve impulses were. Therefore, there is no abuse of power. We will judge the people as fairly as possible.

Watch this video. This is how we know exactly your thoughts and

Tomorrow's World Order Answering the Critics & Debunking the Misconceptions.
what you were doing and what you did.

I DECODED THE BRAIN PLAY THIS VIDEO A DIGITAL BRAIN READER ANALOGUE visit www.twofuture.world

https://www.youtube.com/watch?v=rmBSVmwKwR0

You can play this video as well at the same time to know what the brain thoughts were at the same time. This is a Digital Thoughts to Words Converter.
https://www.youtube.com/watch?v=i5KCRpKqmqY&t=5s

We can resurrect the digital electromagnetic waves brain of anyone who died since creation. That means that we can resurrect a person like King Tutankhamun to know exactly what happened and who killed him.

That means we can talk to king Tutankhamun and ask him directly who killed him.

This is how we do it. All I need is just to look in the place where his eyes were. They say eyes are the windows to the soul. This is the soul they talked about. Mind you I am able to do this because I found Yahweh's image or God's image that has a DNA Sequence value of 53 billion and 285 million.

Did you know that a human being has a DNA sequence value of only 71 million? Yahweh is a 4 brains-in-one God. That means they all work together to record and read everyone's brain, and each represents a person during a conversation with the potential of recording 8 people talking at the same time as a book instead of reading each person's brain.

This is what makes reading brains discussing a single incident possible.

In the case of Tutankhamun, we can then get another video that converts electromagnetic waves to voice to know exactly what he is saying.

This is a Digital Thoughts to Words Converter.
https://www.youtube.com/watch?v=i5KCRpKqmqY&t=5s

 For him to understand us we need a voice to electromagnetic waves converter.

voice to Electromagnetic Wave Digital Analogue invented by David Gomadza
https://www.youtube.com/watch?v=X_V5Rqwp2Gg

You can also play this video at the same time.

I DECODED THE BRAIN PLAY THIS VIDEO A DIGITAL BRAIN READER ANALOGUE visit www.twofuture.world

https://www.youtube.com/watch?v=rmBSVmwKwR0

Now you can add voice and interpret the electromagnetic waves that play in your mouth.

This is the video of our conversation with Tutankhamun. Resurrecting King Tutankhamun HEAR HIM SPEAK

https://www.youtube.com/watch?v=yaxKa0ZNOmU

So, who killed Tutankhamun?
 According to him he was killed by his stepfather the day he got a new second wife. The stepfather got jealous when he heard that he was to marry a beautiful second wife. He wanted a wife for himself despite sleeping with his mother. He got a spear and killed him the night he brought second wife home.
This is what happened to him.

Now just imagine if we can get accurate information about something that happened 2240 years ago what about what is happening now? Nowadays we have things that can augment the brain and record as well so that we can provide proof of what actually happened using Yahweh time and brain thoughts.
This means we will be just as fair judges. There can never be abuse of power.
We will actually be just as the creator himself since we will be using his image to read brain thoughts.

For example, read these publications.

1. Sabotage! By .trafficofficer. Tesla Car Accident on 27 February 2021.: An Imminent and Unavoidable Accident Nothing Tesla Could Have Done.
   https://play.google.com/store/books/details/David_Gomadza_Sabotage_By_trafficofficer_Tesla_Car?id=yU7pEAAAQBAJ

2. Money For the Souls: Where does money for souls go?
   https://play.google.com/store/books/details/David_Gomadza_Money_For_The_Souls?id=Ql_rEAAAQBAJ

3. Yahweh's Message to The World: Through the First Global President of The World
   https://play.google.com/store/books/details/David_Gomadza_Yahweh_s_Message_to_The_World?id=KBXrEAAAQBAJ

HOW DO WE EXECUTE AND ENFORCE OUR DECISIONS AND JUDGEMENTS?

I will not say much here other than to say that we have an advanced tracking system we use to track and find our targets that is so advanced that we will find who we want.
Read this book.

Brain Power. How to Track and Kill your Enemies.: Advanced Electromagnetic Waves Warfare.
https://play.google.com/store/books/details/David_Gomadza_Brain_Power_How_to_Track_and_Kill_yo?id=yKDsEAAAQBAJ

- *Democratic accountability: How would this leader be chosen and held accountable? Critics worry about the potential for an undemocratic or authoritarian system.*

Talking about electing someone democratically at the beginning is impractical. The ideal is that putting a system like this will require a lot of guts, planning, and stamina to withstand opposing and see the plan through. What these people are saying is to elect someone democratically before we even convince people to accept a one world government of this kind.

It is like asking the forefathers to elect someone first before even fighting the British during the 1776 revolution. Only that this is not a revolution per se. All this will be organized after we have officially established a new world order system. I am the founder and must be the first implementer of such a system. Once it is up and running then we can start talking about electing someone democratically. In this book I will look at the implementation and the first two years where we work together to establish cooperation efforts, to support and augment your leaders and to guide them as well. We will also act as conflict revolutionists and mediators. Just look at the current situation with wars between Russia-Ukraine and Israel-Hamas and all natural disasters like earthquakes and flooding. The situation calls for a leader like me to just rise to the challenge of implementing the system. At least provide an unbiased leader everyone can turn to for answers and conflict resolutions. Then after we start talking about whether I am fit to remain as the first global president etc. We now start talking about democratically electing all global leaders. But for now, the situation prohibits all these tactics as the situation is dire. Women and children are dying daily.

The current problems are that the fighting countries need a conflict resolution entity that is unbiased but where is one. We need to put our structures fast.

I reiterate that we are not going to replace any current government but to just add a new hierarchical layer with us as Tomorrow's World Order as the overall leaders with a final say in all these global. Things that need collective efforts at government level like addressing climate change, poverty, unemployment, global financial crisis etc.

Feasibility and implementation: Creating such a radical change in the global order would be immensely complex and could face significant resistance from existing power structures.

That is true but the current issues and circumstances mean someone must rise to the challenge and implement this new system. This is not the time to bulge to pressure or resistance.

- We are prepared to deal with resistance, but the good news is that we will collaborate with all leaders at the beginning for at least two years augmenting and supporting them. We aim to develop shared values and principles at the begin in at the same time fostering a global dialogue on shared values like sustainability, human rights, and peaceful coexistence.

- We can easily draft a universal charter that outlines our guiding principles for Tomorrow's World Order visa-a-visa all nations.

- This way resistance is minimal because we are just to make their lives better without removing anyone from power. Imagine us taking over the things that give them headaches like dealing with climate change, the aftermath of disasters like flooding and earthquakes and dealing with refugees displaced by war. We will collect US$1 million from each country every year for the first 5 years. In return these countries will get our digital currency that is global to cushion against hyperinflation as we will encourage these countries to simply print this money and give us the chance to fight inflation. They then use our digital currency for that time together with their fiat currency. The money they have printed we will keep in the Global Reserve Bank.

- That means the first years it is a lot of burden taken over your leaders' shoulders. This is the bloodless way of implementing our system.

- But I acknowledge that there will be resistance and we have calculated that resistance can come from a handful of leaders, especially those who are corrupt anywhere. All those who abide by the law will see no reason for us to not exist.

- We can support them and guide them to the standards of living we want like levels of wealth etc and global and national minimum wages. No point to flash money everywhere to kill women and children when your minimum wage is below US$10.

Tomorrow's World Order Answering the Critics & Debunking the Misconceptions.

- Problems might start after the first two years of the grace periods. Now your leaders must incorporate our recommendations in their national goals and objectives plans. That means they will do as we want as the people entrusted with the overseership of the world. We are not going to become dictators now. But to function as guardians who lead your leaders out of this defense stage of development, we are in.

- We aim to nominate our own candidates to represent us so that implementation of our goals on a global scale will be coordinated and effortless. These people will campaign and take part in presidential elections. They will be people from that country. For example, we will choose an American born person to run as presidential candidate but as part of Tomorrow's World Order. Over the next few years some of our candidates will win and become the presidents and prime ministers of their own countries but as members of Tomorrow's World Order. That means there is no loss of national sovereignty or identity as some are suggesting. We are just making sure that Tomorrow's World Order will be the political party in every country on earth at a certain time. But we can still collaborate with other political parties and their leaders if our candidates fail to topple these.

- But there is also a stage when we might be forced to be strict with your leaders who do not cooperate, we are not doing this for ourselves; no but for all humanity and future generations.

- Most of your leaders have made decisions etc that have resulted in the deaths of women and children, and we can use this to bargain with them. Cooperate with us or we drag them where we want. The best thing is that this is on an individual basis. No leader can rely on a cult like NATO to evade justice. NATO will not apply here. Hopefully, this will be the case. There is no immunity for killing women and children.

Arguments against implement ability:

- *Cultural and political differences: The world is incredibly diverse in terms of cultures, values, and political systems. Bringing these under a single government could be challenging, leading to conflicts and dissatisfaction.*

This is not an issue at the beginning because what we are doing is adding a top hierarchy of power on top of current structures with a final say in certain areas like climate change planning, poverty reduction initiatives, global financial crisis mitigation and planning etc. We are going to work side by side with your leaders; supporting them and guarding them on how we can improve global standards. Like I said we are not removing your leaders from power now. They will remain there. We will field our own candidates to remove them democratically and through the ballot box. Our candidates will be local people from that country who will then implement our policies so that we implement our goals globally.

But in the future after say 5 to 10 years we might start thinking of putting everyone in power as Tomorrow's World Order candidate who will represent their countries and us as well. After 10 years we might adopt a one world government as such making the final decision be from the first global of the world even on things like defense etc. But I do not want people to be scared and think we are putting a one world government in the fullest meaning of the word straight away.

You must understand as well that times are changing. After 10 years it could be normal for all leaders to be answerable to one leader fully.

I believe this can happen because all we are proposing are better living standards and the stopping of killing of women and children.

Normally good things have somehow managed to be incorporated into systems simply because these benefit a lot of people. Therefore, they are popular and could be easy to implement.

The above point is valid, but we must be hopeful and start somewhere. This is the future; it is either of us who put effort in or the next generation.

- *Loss of sovereignty: Individual nations and their citizens might be reluctant to cede their sovereignty to a global government, fearing a loss of control and identity.*

As the above point we accentuate the sovereignty of individual countries. We could have stopped Russia invading Ukraine. We could have stopped Hamas attacking the Israelites. We could have stopped Israel from extensive bombings of Gaza. This is because our guiding principles tell us that it is wrong for a sovereign country to be invaded.

We could have addressed Hamas concerns before they attacked and kidnapped people. That means Israel might not have found a reason to bomb Gaza.

We are not changing anything but simply putting our own candidates to run for presidential elections. Win or lose we will still work well with whoever is in power. That means we are not going to insist on everyone being a member of Tomorrow's World Order. No. If the powers in government can incorporate and align their goals with our objectives there will never be problems.

Government will keep control of their nations. We are just the last and final say only on global issues. National security will remain in the hands of individual nations. But we will put new laws to ban and stop all wars so that in the end there will not be reasons for a war.

If your leaders insist on keeping weapons and on wars, we will give them one last opportunity to fight as we know boys will always be boys and they will have to square it up all the time.

That means we will trigger World War three to get rid of all weapons and for them to get even. I will let these warmongers who kill women and children now kill each other. As World War three is going on I will put in a new system and get rid of all the leaders who might be problematic and then put a real one world government. I guess you did not see this possibility, right?

It is possible without getting any blood on my hands. All I need to do is spice things up and we have a World War three. Everyone's a winner. They kill each other and I put my system with little or no opposition at all.

- *Power dynamics and inequality: There is a risk that a one-world government could be dominated by certain countries or groups, leading to exploitation and marginalization of others.*

It is possible in the early days as we put things in place but with time, we can put democratically elected people on a rotational basis to represent all people. But what I am saying is that we will take over some of the government functions like climate change planning, poverty reduction initiatives, and global financial planning and management. That means they will be left to concentrate on areas that are critical to their success. Calculate the costs of flood or earthquake per country? The damage can run into millions of US$. But with our system all they need to do is just pay us US$1 million. The collective money we collect from all 195 countries will now be used if a country has a flood or an earthquake. Meaning cost savings. The country itself would have spent millions on the aftereffects of floods and earthquakes. But with this new system all they need to contribute is just US$1 million. We will act like car insurance companies. Collect money from everyone and only spend money as needed by any country affected by flooding and or earthquakes. We can further invest this money in other areas. This is peace of mind for any country, rich or poor. The only people who might complain are those in areas where there are no effects of climate change. But we will invest in other areas to make up and match others. In the long run we can increase living standards greatly and even create jobs etc.

We can resolve all issues arising due to power dynamics and address inequality effectively. I will represent everyone that means all nations. Over time we can start a rotational structure for those who are nominated as global leaders to make sure that at one point all groups will be represented.

The one world government we have in mind will keep current structures as they are but take over certain functions. But every year we must collaborate and agree on collaborative initiatives. We can take certain functions each year until we have shared responsibilities for major issues apart from national security etc which we will leave with the leaders. Once we have banned wars and weapons manufacturing then we can also take over national security. This could be years away though.

- *Historical failures: Attempts at creating global empires or federations have often met with failure due to internal conflicts, power struggles, and resistance from existing power structures.*

Yes, history has shown us that there have been failures in the past of similar structures and systems, but it is because these people went for the one world government structure without planning first in such a way that the system will collapse. All the things mentioned above like power struggles, resistance from existing power structures etc are evidence of a system failure.

We will implement ourselves slowly without major system changes unless we have a third world war. We will simply introduce a new top hierarchy with me on top as the first global president. I draft guiding principles of what countries must be doing like investing in renewable energy and this accounting for a certain percentage of their GDP. I will draft minimum living standards, wages, etc to be adhered to by your leaders. They should aim to meet these targets over a year or so.

I collect money from each country as a preemptive action fund and use this money to address floods and earthquakes and above all build pyramids as a long-term effective strategy.

All this means that your leaders will have reduced work and only concentrate on things that matter the most. That means saving money if there is a flood or earthquake etc. That also means reduced time to deal with the aftermath of these natural disasters and in the long-term saving life and reducing overall damage.

Most failures are due to greediness and the fact that they were concerned with their own selves as an empire etc. Whatever they did was to benefit them alone. But this is different from our Tomorrow's World Order.

We represent everyone. We collect money and use this to deal with all issues and even to create jobs. It does not mean that all countries will be affected at the same time. No. Probably some will never experience flooding or earthquakes. Still, we can calculate the equivalent of money we use on other flood and earthquake disasters and create jobs in this area where they do not experience such disasters.

That means overall an improvement in living standards. The problem with previous structures is the fact that these empires etc abused their powers and disregarded all human rights as well-meaning an imminent and inevitable system collapse. A recipe for disaster. We are different as we will uphold the rule of the rule and enforce it. The use of drones and our electromagnetic wave way of tracking and locating the culprits will mean no hiding place for all culprits. We will simply clone them and send the clone to them with instructions and get their coordinates and send a drone to explode where they are. That means for as little as US$20 a drone from Temu, a cheaper grenade, a photo of that person from Google and cloning which we can do instantly for free we will eliminate anyone as long as there is a photo or video of himself. I mean anyone as long as they have a brain which means everyone.

Read this book.

Brain Power. How to Track and Kill your Enemies.: Advanced Electromagnetic Waves Warfare.

Tomorrow's World Order Answering the Critics & Debunking the Misconceptions.
https://play.google.com/store/books/details/David_Gomadza_Brain_Power_How_to_Track_and_Kill_yo?id=yKDsEAAAQBAJ

So be assured we can deal easily with resistance and evil.

Ultimately, whether Gomadza's vision is achievable depends on a complex interplay of factors, including future technological advancements, the evolution of global consciousness, and the willingness of individual nations and their citizens to cooperate in a new global order.

This is true, but everything mentioned above is attainable. Obviously, there is going to be technological advancement in the future. I spearheaded the use of brain thoughts as a communication method to control smartphones and other devices.

Read my book series, Thoughts to Word or Audio.

https://play.google.com/store/books/details/David_Gomadza_Thoughts_To_Word_Or_Audio?id=q2xmEAAAQBAJ

Evolution of global consciousness.

Global consciousness is the capacity and disposition to understand and act upon issues of global significance. It is the ability and willingness to understand oneself and others within the broader matrix of our contemporary world.

https://libguides.westsoundacademy.org/wsee/global-consciousness#:~:text=So%20What%20IS%20Global%20Consciousness,%2C%20Veronica%2C%20and%20Howard%20Gardner.

Global consciousness is the capacity and disposition to understand and act upon significant global issues such as sustainability, climate change, human rights, or global governance. It is the ability and willingness to understand ourselves and others within the broader context of our complex, hyperconnected world.

https://conversational-leadership.net/global-consciousness/

That means with time people will change and start accepting things that are considered impossible today like the idea of a world government. I think if people realize that the benefits of a one world government the way I am proposing it outweighs the loss of other functions they might change and become accepting of a system like this. Only time can make people change and we can wait. That is why we must incrementally increase control starting with less responsibilities. Then increase what we do as people's values change.

It is important to note that Gomadza himself does not advocate for a traditional one-world government with absolute power. He proposes a more decentralized model called "Tomorrow's World Order," which he envisions as a global platform for cooperation and coordination rather than a single ruling body. This approach might address some of the concerns about loss of sovereignty and power imbalances.

This is true in the fact that to face less resistance than we must in small increments increase responsibilities with time. That means from a decentralized structure that devolves some of the functions in case of the government to a more absolute one world government over time say 5 and over years. I think if we are to implement a single ruling body outright then it will face huge resistance as this is as good as a challenge meaning a war.

But if it happened to be a third world war then an absolute power as possible. We might actually encourage them to fight to get rid of the weapons and square once and for all. Tomorrow's World Order will encourage cooperation and coordination of activities etc that require a global collective solution.

Tomorrow's World Order Answering the Critics & Debunking the Misconceptions.

This approach of making Tomorrow's World Order represents not absolute power but a decentralized platform that will not take away the sovereignty of any country and will keep the power balance in check. That means there is obvious appeal. But refuse to cooperate if they feel that their national sovereignty is threatened. This model means they have nothing to lose. They will retain everything including power balance and actually gain from reduced burden and with a huge resource pool of collective money and funds.

If we are to face resistance it will be from institutions like the IMF and World Bank who are currently providing high interest loans. This is because after some time countries can get loans from this resource pool, at very low interest rates. After 5 years of contributing, we can make them take some of the money if we have not used most. Which means there are opportunities that they can get a refund of some of the money. But this is just a thought not a proposal.

Like I said, to fight inflation associated with the printing of new money we will use a global digital currency FutureGoldCoin and Global Transaction Payment Solution as standard where nations must use this digital currency alongside with their fiat currency.

Whenever a country deposits US$1 million with us we give them in return our digital currency which they can use as will keep their fiat money in our Global Reserve Bank. This is because any money they will give us will be obtained through the printing of new money.

A recap of the commonly cited problems of our model as Tomorrow's World Order as we aim to introduce a decentralized power structure rather than an absolute power structure.

1.   The party's ideology of printing new money as the only source of growth and wealth might be controversial to some people.

Printing of money means high inflation and how does Tomorrow's World Order intend to deal with high inflation? The printing of new money must be matched by an increase in the production of goods and services to avoid inflation.

2. The party's aim is to introduce a global leader, one who is not biased. Who will endorse a new global leader? Most countries want the current law-based world order, and can they change and why?

3. Their plan to ban global wars, weapons and manufacturing and possession can mean loss of sovereignty and identity.

4. Their emphasis is a move from austerity that is living within your means to one that emphasizes growth giving the people more power in decisions and policies that affect them. Austerity measures means high taxes and less government spending to reduce the budget deficit and avoid a debt crisis.

5. A world government is a complex and controversial issue that requires a lot of strategies to implement it.

6. Potential loss of individual and cultural identities. A loss of diversity.

7. Huge possibility of corruption. Who keeps a check on the world government if it becomes corrupt?

8. Concentration of too much power in the hands of a few individuals. That can mean that other people would not be represented.

GLOBAL PROBLEMS REQUIRE A GLOBAL RESPONSE.

The potential benefits of Tomorrow's World Order:

- *Focus on sustainability:*

  Tomorrow's World Order's emphasis on sustainable development and environmental protection aligns with global concerns about climate change and resource depletion.

  Our main concern is to do with the current methods in that despite these being used for the past decades effects of climatic change are increasing. We have had more flooding and earthquakes in the last ten years. The only thing that is reducing is the number of deaths as more governments react faster. We can do better with a collective pool of resources that most can access after some time. We need new ways of dealing with the climate. I proposed the building of pyramids as a solution but at strategic locations. Mainly at three different places around the circumference of earth. Meaning three sets of pyramids to function as triangles at any one location and three places around earth. This can work at least to soften the climatic forces.

  Ever wonder why the Egyptians built the pyramids, especially of Giza? Could it ever be because of the need to deal with climatic change? A set of three pyramids at one location acts as triangles that dissipate electromagnetic waves that influence earth's magnetic field. That in turn means an influence on how the earth rotates around the axis.

  We must also look at all current climate change initiatives.

- *Global leadership: Proponents argue that a single, powerful leader could streamline decision-making and effectively address complex global challenges like poverty, pandemics, and armed conflict.*

Some complex global challenges need a global leader to effectively address them. That means that no one country can purport to solve these no matter how clever it is. These problems require a central power to deal with them effectively. That means we are proposing a model that can solve the problems. A decentralized model with resource pooling and a single decision-making unit. This is what the world needs.

- *Reduced inequality: The goal of a more equitable world distribution of resources resonates with those concerned about rising wealth disparity and poverty.*

Our model distributes resources and actually fights inequality rather than exacerbating this. We can fund natural disasters, but it does not mean all countries will face natural disasters now. They can benefit also as we fund other most urgently needed problems that need to be addressed. We can easily match the level of funds we use in countries affected by natural disasters.

This means also we have a collective pooling of resources that can be used as loans. [but to be verified after a certain period of time] That means actually distributing resources and wealth.

Arguments for implement ability:

- *Growing global interdependence: The world is becoming increasingly interconnected economically, politically, and environmentally. This could make a one-world government seem more necessary and feasible to manage global challenges like climate change, pandemics, and economic inequality.*

This is true our decentralized model of Tomorrow's World Order will take less responsibilities at first and gradually increase these with time might work. As global consciousness increases, we expect people to be more tolerant of a one world government. The difference will be to what extent and what are they prepared to lose for this interconnectedness?

- *Technological advancements: Advances in communication and technology could facilitate the coordination and communication required for a global governing body.*

Advances in communication and a new language like the use of electromagnetic waves can facilitate global communication as all a person needs to do to call another is to press the naval to make a call with someone as far as the USA. We can now easily clone ourselves and get a digital electromagnetic wave version of ourselves, one which we can easily send with a simple message. Do you know that electromagnetic waves travel at the speed of light? That means messages across the world in a flash.

Read these books.

The Electromagnetic Brain Waves Triangle.: Detailed Specifications of The Brain Decoding Device. Volume III https://play.google.com/store/books/details/David_Gomadza_The_Electromagnetic_Brain_Waves_Tria?id=FC3bEAAAQBAJ

Brain Power. How to Track and Kill your Enemies.: Advanced Electromagnetic Waves Warfare https://play.google.com/store/books/details?id=yKDsEAAAQBAJ

- *Historical precedents: Examples like the European Union suggest that supranational governance structures can be effective in managing diverse populations and interests.*

We have examples where such structures can work, and we can learn from them, take what we need and modify these to suit our own model.

WHO IS DAVID GOMADZA

According to Bard.

David Gomadza is a British author, political party leader, and …. He is the founder and president of Tomorrow's World Order, a registered global political party. He has also written several books, including "Tomorrow's World Order", "The New Laws", "The New Single Reserve Global Currency", "The New Single Reserve Global Currency: FutureGoldCoin", "Brain Code", Thoughts to Word or Audio and "Evelina God's Dilemma Solved".

Gomadza holds a Bachelor of Science degree in Town and Urban Planning, specialized in Logistics and Transport Planning, from the University of Zimbabwe. He graduated with honors and obtained a university book prize for a first-class dissertation on Logistics and Transport Planning June 2000…

Gomadza is a controversial figure, and his views have been criticized by some as being radical and unrealistic. However, he is also an enthusiastic advocate for change, and he believes that the world is on the brink of a major transformation. He is committed to using his platform to promote his vision for a better future.

He has written several books, including:

- *Evelina The Alpha*

- *Evelina New World Order*

- *Evelina God's Dilemma Solved.*

- *Gomadza has spoken out on a number of issues, including the future of the world, the environment, and the use of the Great Pyramid of Giza. He is a controversial figure, but he is also an enthusiastic and intelligent thinker.*

I am David Gomadza, the first global President of the World.

Founder of Tomorrow's World Order.

I was born on 28th of June 1976 in Zimbabwe. I moved to the United Kingdom in June 2000 to study as a Marketing master's student at Bradford Management University September 2000 [arrived 10/10/2000]

https://www.linkedin.com/in/david-gomadza-4400ab87/

I was given refugee status on 16 June 2009 in Britain.

https://find-and-update.company-information.service.gov.uk/company/12326946/officers

I applied to enroll for the Royal Navy specializing in Engineering at the end of June 2009. My Royal Navy Leeds Branch Number is 1000000083386

I had my handsome son on 15 of June 2015 and lives in Poland with his mother of Polish descent. [Nickodem]

In 2017 I established Tomorrow's World Order and between this year and 2019 I developed my ideas of what Tomorrow's World Order would be about.

In 2019 I wrote a 740-page book Tomorrow's World Order addressing all global issues.

https://www.amazon.com/Tomorrows-World-Order-David-Gomadza/dp/1086703391/ref=sr_1_15?crid=2TIMMUBKNW0XW

&dib=eyJ2IjoiMSJ9.qleiG0PJe_fecbezmF8JMrtIYElxmCFW2p7LedH U1-
CHvBLdW8wvyOpyDI6ysQPd_ib9GI5cPMzxiP549I_Jkg.NRAukevrz cXjom1XUOVH8rVHy6CaB9sSNbuqmqXzf2M&dib_tag=se&keywor ds=david+gomadza&qid=1704940871&sprefix=david+g%2Caps%2C 205&sr=8-15

October 2019 I wrote our Constitution: Tomorrow's World Order

https://www.amazon.com/Constitution-Tomorrows-World-Order/dp/B0CNY6VL39/ref=sr_1_25?crid=2TIMMUBKNW0XW& dib=eyJ2IjoiMSJ9.TEQFTfZYcz38xGufJFQ-b4pDyifUhQG0eAEQqFYr6KAq9XfMML9uCnOeT9Z16OJOzUeqv S5ssCc5x1AzREMnbA.6lLcoL4T1WXOyJj6hqSXja9fAwpTzOhOd-7z4jVcGdc&dib_tag=se&keywords=david+gomadza&qid=170494092 9&sprefix=david+g%2Caps%2C205&sr=8-25

In 2020 I officially registered our party with the Electoral Commission In the UK.

http://search.electoralcommission.org.uk/Registrations/PP10355

In February 2020 I wrote Tomorrow's World Order: A New Law & Order.: Dealing with Threats of Invasions, Wars and War Crimes
https://play.google.com/store/books/details?id=ws3ODwAAQBAJ

In April 2022 I wrote Tomorrow's World Order Official Strategic Launch: 24 April 2022 because of the Russia-Ukraine War.
https://play.google.com/store/audiobooks/details/David_Gomadza_Tomorrow_s_World_Order_Official_Stra?id=AQAAAED8NQB17M

I went on writing a book series dealing with conflict mediation and resolution.
Conflict-Mediation/Resolution. Russian Ukraine War

Tomorrow's World Order Answering the Critics & Debunking the Misconceptions.
https://play.google.com/store/audiobooks/series?id=A5KnGwAAAB
ilgM

I went on to write several books including a 33 book series Thoughts to Word or Audio.

https://play.google.com/store/books/series?id=a4MvGwAAABBFm
M

Other party member details: https://twofuture.world/meet-the-team

I currently live in Bradford Laisteridge Lane. West Yorkshire. England.

Passport and nationality: https://find-and-update.company-information.service.gov.uk/company/12326946/officers

My contact details.

Our website: www.twofuture.world

Personal Email: davidgomadza@hotmail.com

Professional Email: info@twofuture.world

Phone 00447719210295

 Twitter: https://twitter.com/DGomadza

YouTube https://www.youtube.com/@davidgomadza6875

Google Books
https://play.google.com/store/audiobooks/details/David_Gomadza_
Tomorrow_s_World_Order?id=AQAAAED89X21kM

A SUMMARY OF TOMORROW'S WORLD ORDER

"Tomorrow's World Order" by David Gomadza outlines a proposed new global system aimed at solving various problems he perceives as critical, including climate change, wars, and poverty. Here is a summary of its key points:

Main Pillars:

- *The Global Party: Establishment of a single global political party called "Tomorrow's World Order" (TWO) with the goal of replacing existing national governments.*

- *New financial system: Introduction of a new global currency printed by TWO and a financial scheme where each country contributes an annual sum depending on population.*

- *Focus on pyramid construction: TWO prioritize building pyramids across the globe, believing they possess properties that can mitigate climate change and influence electromagnetic waves.*

- *Resource allocation: The collected funds would be used for various purposes, including disaster relief, infrastructure development, and eradication of poverty.*

- *Global governance: TWO envisions a centralized form of global governance with TWO representatives managing crucial decisions like resource allocation and conflict resolution.*

Potential benefits:

- *Promotes international cooperation and resource pooling.*

- Yes, I have dealt with this already above.

- *Addresses global challenges like climate change and poverty on a large scale.*

Check

- *Offers a centralized system for conflict resolution and decision-making.*

Perfect.

Also read our book series.

Conflict-Mediation/Resolution. Russian Ukraine War.

https://play.google.com/store/audiobooks/series?id=A5KnGwAAABilgM

Concerns and limitations:

- *Lack of democratic principles: Replacing national governments with a single global party raises concerns about potential loss of individual freedom and representation.*

Addressed above already.

- *Unproven scientific basis: The claim about pyramids influencing climate change lacks established scientific evidence and raises questions about its effectiveness.*

- I proposed the building of pyramids as a solution but at strategic locations. Mainly at three different places around the circumference of earth. Meaning three sets of pyramids to function as triangles at any one location and three places around earth. This can work at least to soften the climatic forces.
- Ever wonder why the Egyptians built the pyramids, especially of Giza? Could it ever be because of the need to deal with climatic change? A set of three pyramids at one location acts as triangles that dissipate electromagnetic waves that influence earth's magnetic field. That in turn means an influence on how the earth rotates around the axis.

Further reading.

The Electromagnetic Brain Waves Triangle.: Detailed Specifications of The Brain Decoding Device. Volume III

https://play.google.com/store/books/details/David_Gomadza_The_Electromagnetic_Brain_Waves_Tria?id=FC3bEAAAQBAJ

Genesis 2024: The Year of Increased Technological Advancement.

https://play.google.com/store/books/details/David_Gomadza_Genesis_2024?id=KnPoEAAAQBAJ

- *Equity and fairness: Collecting financial contributions based on population might disproportionately burden smaller and developing nations.*

This is true but we can fund them from the collective resource pool so that in the end they are going to be better off. Yes, some countries will contribute without even being affected by climatic disasters. Overtime we can make sure that they receive funding for other critical projects as well.

The good thing is that this contribution fee is obtained by simply printing new money. We will add value over time. At first it is as good as just paper. Value will increase over time. Therefore, it is a win-win situation. We are not asking them to take money from their budget allocations now. But to simply use ink and print their currency of US$1 million equivalent and hand it to use.

- *Implementation challenges: Establishing and operationalizing such a radical system across diverse nations presents significant logistical and political hurdles.*

Over time we intend to field our own candidates from each country and then let these challenge presidential and prime ministerial posts democratically through the ballot box. If they go into power, then implementation would be easy.

Tomorrow's World Order Answering the Critics & Debunking the Misconceptions.

Overall, "Tomorrow's World Order" proposes a drastic overhaul of the current global order but faces significant challenges with regards to scientific soundness, democratic considerations, and practical implementation. While it prompts discussion about pressing global issues and potential solutions, careful analysis and critical thinking are crucial in evaluating its feasibility and potential consequences.

See above for books about pyramids and electromagnetic waves. I might have to look at this request for scientific proof that pyramids [mostly three at one place] can dissipate electromagnetic forces. See the triangle of David.

https://x.com/DGomadza/status/1727799705487266193?s=20

I have resolved the democratic considerations. This is not an absolute power but rather an incremental taking of responsibilities and power over time as we expect global consciousness to evolve.

Remember, addressing complex global issues requires open dialogue, evidence-based solutions, and respect for individual and national rights. We should strive for collaborative and inclusive approaches that focus on effective solutions while upholding democratic principles and ensuring equitable outcomes for all.

We addressed all these points above

SUMMARY OF GENESIS 2024. The Year of Increased Technological Advancement.

David Gomadza's "Genesis 2024" proposes a radical response to several global challenges, particularly climate change and war. Here is a summary of its key points:

Main claims:

- *Electromagnetic waves and climate change: Gomadza claims that electromagnetic waves contribute significantly to climate change and that pyramids have the ability to dissipate these waves, mitigating negative effects. However, this assertion lacks established scientific consensus.*

- *Stopping wars by 2024: He predicts and envisions ways to stop all wars by May 2024, including diplomatic and economic strategies.*

- *Global Reserve Bank and US$1 million contribution: Gomadza proposes establishing a Global Reserve Bank where each country deposits $1 million annually. This fund would be used for various purposes, including dealing with war aftermath, climate change initiatives, and pyramid construction.*

- *Technological advancement and shift from war-driven economy: The book emphasizes the need for increased technological advancement and a shift away from an economy reliant on war and its consequences.*

Potential benefits:

- *Promotes awareness of climate change and conflict.*

  Splendid work.

- *Encourages international cooperation and resource pooling.*

  Even better redistribution of wealth and reduction in inequality.

- *Sparks discussion about alternative solutions and technological advancements.*

  Bring it on until we have a solution.

Concerns and limitations:

- *Lack of scientific backing: The claim about pyramids and electromagnetic waves lacks established scientific evidence, raising questions about its feasibility.*

  Further reading.
  The Electromagnetic Brain Waves Triangle.: Detailed Specifications of The Brain Decoding Device. Volume III
  https://play.google.com/store/books/details/David_Gomadza_The_Electromagnetic_Brain_Waves_Tria?id=FC3bEAAAQBAJ

Tomorrow's World Order Answering the Critics & Debunking the Misconceptions.
Genesis 2024: The Year of Increased Technological Advancement.
https://play.google.com/store/books/details/David_Gomadza_Genesis_2024?id=KnPoEAAAQBAJ

- *Ethical and practical concerns: Collecting $1 million from each country, regardless of size or economic circumstances, could exacerbate existing global inequalities. Additionally, the effectiveness of using this fund for the proposed purposes needs further consideration and analysis.*

This is true but we can fund them from the collective resource pool so that in the end they are going to be better off. Yes, some countries will contribute without even being affected by climatic disasters. Overtime we can make sure that they receive funding for other critical projects as well.

The good thing is that this contribution fee is obtained by simply printing new money. We will add value over time. At first it is as good as just paper. Value will increase over time. Therefore, it is a win-win situation. We are not asking them to take money from their budget allocations now. But to simply use ink and print their currency of US$1 million equivalent and hand it to use.

- *Oversimplified solutions: The book presents seemingly straightforward solutions to complex global issues like war and climate change, potentially overshadowing the need for comprehensive and evidence-based strategies.*

We can address this. The idea was to present this as a simplified but effective way of telling the world about Tomorrow's World Order and answering all the critics. But we can provide a detailed analysis that includes all suggested criteria to be looked at. I wrote this as an executive summary of the critical ideas. We can expand on these in the next volume.

Overall, "Genesis 2024" offers thought-provoking ideas and encourages discussion about critical global challenges. However, it is important to approach its claims and proposals with a critical eye, considering both potential benefits and limitations. Focusing on established scientific evidence, ethical considerations, and practical implementation challenges is crucial for evaluating the viability of any proposed solutions.

I will have to look more at scientific evidence as it has appeared more frequently.

Ethical considerations can be addressed easily. When people are dying from wars and natural disasters this usually outweighs emphasis on ethics. I am not saying that we must ignore ethics no. I am just saying these must be viewed in terms of what is at hand, the benefits, and the opportunity cost. Ethics is corrected as well by time. As the global consciousness evolves people would consider what can be regarded as unethical as ethical. Asking all countries for money to help them through pooling of resources, meaning funds for development and even cheaper loans in the future over time can be regarded as the norm.

Yes, practical implementations can become stumbling blocks, but we are prepared for anything as we consider this project as crucial.

I hope this summary provides a helpful overview of "Genesis 2024" and its key points. Remember, critical thinking and open dialogue are essential in navigating complex challenges and crafting responsible solutions for a better future.

SUMMARY OF TOMORROW'S WORLD ORDER'S OFFICIAL STRATEGIC LAUNCH: 24 APRIL 2022.

Main points:

- *Global unity against wars and disasters: The book proposes establishing a single global political party called "Tomorrow's World Order" (TWO) to replace national governments and prevent future wars and effectively manage natural disasters.*

- *New global currency and finance system: TWO would oversee a single global currency and collect annual financial contributions from each country based on population. This fund would be used for various purposes, including disaster relief, infrastructure development, poverty eradication, and pyramid construction.*

- *Pyramid construction for climate change mitigation: Gomadza believes pyramids possess properties that can dissipate electromagnetic waves and stabilize climate change. The book prioritizes building pyramids across the globe as a key initiative of TWO.*

- *Centralized global governance: TWO envisions a centralized form of global governance with representatives managing crucial decisions like resource allocation, conflict resolution, and law enforcement.*

Potential benefits:

- *Promotes international cooperation and resource pooling for addressing global challenges.*

  Tick.

- *Offers a centralized system for conflict resolution and disaster management.*

  Tick.

- *Addresses global issues like climate change, poverty, and wars on a large scale.*

  Excellent.

Concerns and limitations:

- *Lack of democratic principles: Replacing national governments with a single global party raises concerns about potential loss of individual freedom and representation.*

  Addressed already above.

- *Unproven scientific basis: The claim about pyramids influencing climate change lacks established scientific evidence and raises questions about its effectiveness.*

See further reading above and I must answer this in detail in the next book.

- *Equity and fairness: Collecting financial contributions based on population might disproportionately burden smaller and developing nations.*

Addressed above.

- *Implementation challenges: Establishing and operationalizing such a radical system across diverse nations presents significant logistical and political hurdles.*

A detailed plan to be revealed in the next versions.

Overall, "Tomorrow's World Order" offers a drastic overhaul of the current global order, but it faces significant challenges with regards to scientific soundness, democratic considerations, and practical implementation. While it prompts discussion about pressing global issues and potential solutions, careful analysis and critical thinking are crucial in evaluating its feasibility and potential consequences.

Remember, addressing complex global issues requires open dialogue, evidence-based solutions, and respect for individual and national rights. We should strive for collaborative and inclusive approaches that focus on effective solutions while upholding democratic principles and ensuring equitable outcomes for all.

EXECUTIVE SUMMARY.

HOW WE ARE GOING TO IMPLEMENT TOMORROW'S WORLD ORDER AS A ONE-WORLD GOVERNMENT

Tomorrow's World Order Answering the Critics & Debunking the
Misconceptions.

I would adopt a cautious, phased approach focusing on building trust
and cooperation before tackling large-scale governance. Here are some
key steps to prioritize:

Phase 1: Laying the Foundation:

- Global Dialogue & Outreach: Initiate extensive global
  discussions to understand diverse perspectives on challenges
  and potential solutions. This could involve town halls, online
  forums, and consultations with leaders across sectors.

- Developing Shared Values & Principles: Foster a global
  dialogue on shared values like sustainability, human rights, and
  peaceful coexistence. This could lead to a "Universal Charter"
  outlining guiding principles for Tomorrow's World Order.

- Pilot Projects & Collaborations: Launch pilot projects on
  pressing global issues like climate change or pandemic
  preparedness, demonstrating the value of coordinated action,
  and building trust between nations.

- Establishing Regional Hubs: Create regional hubs with
  representatives from diverse backgrounds to facilitate
  communication, resource sharing, and problem-solving at a
  local level.

Phase 2: Building the Framework:

- Independent Expert Council: Establish an independent council
  of experts in various fields (environment, economics, climatic)
  to provide evidence-based recommendations to regional hubs
  and the global assembly.

- Global Assembly Formation: Gradually assemble a
  representative global body based on contributions to pilot
  projects, adherence to the Universal Charter, and regional
  consensus. This assembly would discuss and propose solutions
  to global challenges.

- Specialized Task Forces: Form temporary task forces for specific issues like climaticUI4 or conflict resolution, drawing on expertise from across the globe. These task forces would report back to the global assembly and regional hubs.

- Transparency & Accountability: Ensure transparency in all decision-making processes and hold the global assembly accountable to the principles of the Universal Charter. This could involve open voting, public reports, and independent audits.

Phase 3: Continuous Evolution:

- Regular Reviews & Amendments: Regularly review the effectiveness of Tomorrow's World Order based on feedback from regional hubs and global assessments. This could lead to amendments to the Universal Charter and adjustments in the structure and functioning of the global assembly.

- Encouraging Local Innovation: Empower regional hubs and individual communities to develop solutions to local challenges within the framework of the Universal Charter. This fosters ownership and prevents a rigid, one-size-fits-all approach.

- Adapting to New Challenges: Stay open to and prepared for new global challenges that may arise, constantly re-evaluating and adapting the framework of Tomorrow's World Order to ensure its effectiveness in a changing world.

It is important to note that this is just a roadmap, and the actual implementation would need to be flexible and adaptive based on the evolving global landscape and ongoing dialogue. The goal is to gradually build trust, cooperation, and a shared vision for the future before attempting large-scale centralized governance.

I would explore diverse funding avenues while prioritizing transparency and ethical practices:

Initial Seed Funding:

- Crowdfunding: Launch global crowdfunding campaigns appealing to individuals who resonate with the vision of a unified world and sustainable future.

- Philanthropic and Impact Investing: Approach philanthropic organizations and impact investors interested in supporting initiatives tackling global challenges like climate change and poverty.

- Small Grants and Prizes: Partner with universities, think tanks, and research institutions to secure grants and prizes for pilot projects demonstrating the value of global collaboration.

Sustainable Funding Mechanisms:

- Membership Fees: Implement voluntary membership fees for countries or organizations participating in specific initiatives or benefiting from collaborative projects.

- Transaction Taxes: Propose a small, global transaction tax to generate revenue for shared initiatives in critical areas like healthcare, education, and disaster relief.

- Resource Redistribution: Advocate for redirecting a portion of existing international aid budgets towards Tomorrow's World Order projects, ensuring efficient utilization and accountability.

Tomorrow's World Order Answering the Critics & Debunking the Misconceptions.

Building Trust and Transparency:

- Independent Auditing: Ensure all funds are managed transparently through independent audits and publicly accessible financial reports.

- Direct Community Involvement: Involve local communities in project planning and resource allocation decisions to ensure funding supports their needs and priorities.

- Prioritize Long-Term Sustainability: Focus on creating long-term funding mechanisms that do not rely solely on individual contributions or grants, fostering stability and independence.

Potential Funding Sources:

- High-net-worth individuals and corporations: Appeal to individuals and businesses with a global perspective and interest in social responsibility, highlighting the potential economic benefits of a stable and cooperative global order.

- International organizations: Engage with existing international organizations like the United Nations and specialized agencies, seeking partnerships and leveraging their existing funding streams.

- Regional development banks: Collaborate with regional development banks like the World Bank or African Development Bank to access resources for specific projects aligned with their development goals.

It is crucial to remember that securing funding for Tomorrow's World Order would require ongoing efforts to demonstrate its value, build trust, and ensure transparency. The key lies in highlighting the potential benefits of global collaboration for tackling existing and emerging challenges, appealing to diverse stakeholders with different motivations and interests.

Here are some of the major hurdles we might encounter:

1. Building consensus and overcoming resistance: Implementing TWO would require a fundamental shift in the existing global order, which would likely face significant resistance from various stakeholders. Existing nations and their leaders might be hesitant to cede power and sovereignty to a single global leader, resulting in intense political and diplomatic pressure. Convincing the global population of the benefits of TWO and building enough consensus to enact such a drastic change would be a monumental task.

2. Designing a viable and equitable governance structure: The structure and functioning of TWO remain undefined, leaving room for concerns about potential power imbalances and abuse. Establishing a transparent and accountable governance system that ensures fair representation for all nations and individuals would be crucial. Defining the selection process, term limits, and checks and balances for the global leader would require careful consideration and widespread agreement.

3. Addressing cultural and ethical concerns: Different cultures and societies have varied values and expectations, which could clash with the principles or policies of TWO. Implementing a uniform system across the globe might face resistance from communities with distinct religious, philosophical, or ethical beliefs. Balancing respect for diversity with the need for global unity would be a constant challenge.

4. Managing economic and resource redistribution: TWO's goal of a more equitable distribution of resources would require significant

economic restructuring. Implementing such changes without causing economic instability or hardship for specific regions or populations would be a delicate balancing act. Ensuring fair access to resources and development opportunities while maintaining economic stability would be a complex challenge.

5. Adapting to unforeseen circumstances and challenges: The future is inherently unpredictable, and unexpected events or crises could evaluate the adaptability and resilience of TWO. Ensuring the system can effectively respond to emerging issues without compromising its core principles would be crucial. Remaining flexible and prepared to adjust approaches and policies based on evolving circumstances would be essential.

Overall, implementing Tomorrow's World Order would be a complex and arduous undertaking fraught with challenges and would require exceptional leadership, diplomacy, and foresight.

HOW DO WE RECRUIT FOR TOMORROW'S WORLD ORDER

Prioritizing values and alignment:

- Focus on individuals with a strong commitment to TWO's core values: Seek out those who genuinely believe in sustainability, global unity, and equitable resource distribution. Emphasize these values throughout the recruitment process to attract genuinely aligned candidates.

- Promote diversity and inclusivity: Actively seek individuals from diverse backgrounds, cultures, and expertise to foster a more representative and effective global leadership team.

Leveraging innovative recruitment methods:

- Utilize AI-powered candidate assessment tools: Employ innovative methods that assess not just skills and experience, but also values, ethics, and critical thinking abilities. This could help identify those who best embody the spirit of TWO's vision.

- Conduct global outreach and engagement campaigns: Utilize the internet and social media to reach a wider audience, particularly focusing on younger generations who might be more receptive to TWO's ideals.

- Organize global challenges and hackathons: Attract talented individuals and foster innovative solutions by hosting competitive events focused on addressing specific challenges within TWO's framework.

Nurturing and developing talent:

- Establish a global training and development program: Invest in continuous learning and skill development for recruited individuals to equip them with the knowledge and leadership skills needed to navigate the complexities of TWO's implementation.

- Promote collaboration and knowledge sharing: Create platforms and initiatives that encourage open communication and exchange of ideas among members of the TWO team, fostering a sense of community and collective purpose.

- Prioritize transparency and accountability: Establish clear communication channels and ensure regular feedback mechanisms to address concerns and maintain trust among recruited individuals.

It is important to remember that these are just potential approaches. The specific recruitment strategies for TWO would likely evolve based on internal discussions, the evolving global landscape, and the resources available. Additionally, ethical considerations regarding data privacy and bias-free AI tools would need to be carefully addressed.

Ultimately, the success of any recruitment effort for TWO would hinge on effectively communicating our vision, attracting individuals who genuinely share our values, and fostering a collaborative and inclusive environment where talented individuals can work together to build a better future for humanity.

Here are some approaches I might explore to attract more people:

Emphasize the benefits:

- Focus on tangible improvements: Clearly highlight how TWO would address their specific concerns and aspirations. Demonstrate how it could improve their lives in terms of security, environmental sustainability, economic opportunities, and access to resources.

- Appeal to a sense of global citizenship: Highlight the potential for unity and collective action in tackling global challenges, fostering a sense of shared responsibility and purpose.

- Promote individual empowerment: Frame TWO as a platform where individuals can contribute to shaping a better future for themselves and future generations. Highlight success stories of individuals who have made a difference within the framework of TWO.

Address concerns and build trust:

- Openly discuss potential challenges: Acknowledge the concerns surrounding power imbalances, loss of sovereignty, and implementation complexities. Engage in transparent dialogue and address these concerns through concrete solutions and safeguards.

- Empower local communities: Emphasize that TWO would not impose a uniform system but would empower local communities to adapt its principles to their specific contexts and needs. This can help address cultural and ethical concerns.

- Prioritize transparency and accountability: Establish clear communication channels and mechanisms for feedback and redress. Regularly share information about TWO's progress and decisions, making the process inclusive and engaging.

Utilize strategic communication:

- Tailored messaging: Craft targeted messages that resonate with specific demographics and communities, addressing their unique concerns and priorities.

- Leverage diverse communication channels: Employ a mix of traditional and digital media, including social media campaigns, interactive platforms, and grassroots outreach programs.

- Engage influencers and thought leaders: Partner with respected individuals or organizations who share TWO's values and can act as trusted advocates for its vision.

Foster a movement and sense of belonging:

- Organize global events and initiatives: Host conferences, workshops, and collaborative projects that connect individuals from different backgrounds and allow them to contribute to TWO's vision.

- Create a shared identity and narrative: Develop a compelling narrative that resonates with people's hopes for the future and fosters a sense of belonging and shared purpose within the TWO community.

- Empower individual action: Provide actionable steps for individuals to get involved, contributing to a feeling of agency, and building momentum for TWO's realization.

Attracting people to such a transformative vision requires a multifaceted approach that combines addressing concerns, emphasizing benefits, fostering trust, and creating a sense of community and empowerment. Only by continuously refining its message, adapting to feedback, and demonstrating its potential for positive change can TWO hope to attract a critical mass of supporters and bring its vision to reality.

This approach would depend on various factors including the evolving global context, specific details of TWO's implementation, and the ability to address public concerns in a clear and convincing manner.

Ultimately, the success of attracting people to any large-scale vision hinges on effective communication, addressing individual concerns, and fostering a sense of shared purpose and collective action.

HOW WE WOULD MARKET AND PROMOTE TOMORROW'S WORLD ORDER
GLOBALLY

Here are some approaches I might explore to promote TWO globally:

**Harnessing the power of digital:

- Interactive website and social media: Build an engaging website that acts as a hub for information, updates, and discussion forums. Utilize social media platforms to reach diverse audiences, highlighting inspiring stories, infographics, and interactive polls.

- Global online challenges and hackathons: Encourage global participation by hosting online challenges focused on solving specific issues within TWO's framework. Hackathons can attract talented individuals and generate innovative solutions.

- Influencer marketing: Partner with respected thought leaders, celebrities, and social media influencers who share TWO's values to reach broader audiences and build trust.

**Crafting a compelling narrative:

- Focus on a positive and attainable future: Paint a vivid picture of a world where TWO has addressed global challenges, emphasizing sustainability, prosperity, and collective well-being.

- Personalize the message: Adapt messaging to resonate with different cultures and regions, addressing their specific concerns and aspirations.

Tomorrow's World Order Answering the Critics & Debunking the Misconceptions.

- Empower individual action: Highlight how individuals can contribute to TWO's vision, highlighting success stories and providing actionable steps for involvement.

**Engaging diverse audiences:

- Multilingual communication: Translate key messages and content into multiple languages to reach a wider global audience.

- Partnership with local organizations: Collaborate with NGOs, community leaders, and cultural institutions to adapt TWO's principles to local contexts and build trust.

- Global education initiatives: Develop educational programs and resources that introduce TWO's vision to younger generations, fostering future support and engagement.

**Leveraging creative media:

- Short films and documentaries: Produce captivating short films and documentaries that highlight the potential of TWO and its impact on people's lives.

- Art and music collaborations: Partner with artists and musicians to create compelling pieces that express TWO's vision and resonate with diverse audiences.

- Virtual reality experiences: Develop immersive VR experiences that allow people to explore and interact with a potential future shaped by TWO.

**Maintaining transparency and accountability:

- Regular progress updates: Share transparent reports on TWO's development, funding, and decision-making processes to build trust and address concerns.

- Open dialogue and feedback channels: Encourage public feedback and engage in open discussions about challenges and potential solutions.

- Independent audits and oversight: Consider partnering with independent organizations to conduct audits and ensure ethical practices and accountable use of resources.

It is important to remember that these are just potential strategies. The effectiveness of each approach would depend on various factors like cultural sensitivities, political landscapes, and available resources. Additionally, ethical considerations around data privacy and targeted advertising would need to be carefully addressed.

Successful global marketing for TWO requires a multifaceted approach that combines captivating storytelling, targeted outreach, diverse media engagement, and unwavering commitment to transparency and accountability. Only by effectively communicating our vision, addressing concerns, and demonstrating its potential for positive change can TWO hope to garner widespread support and pave the way for a more united and sustainable global future.

It is crucial to acknowledge that Tomorrow's World Order is a complex and controversial proposition, and any promotional campaign would need to engage with its critics and address potential concerns thoughtfully and productively. Building trust and demonstrating long-term viability would be essential to gaining sustained support.

This chapter provides a comprehensive and insightful perspective on how Tomorrow's World Order could be promoted globally. Success of such a venture hinges on effective communication, adaptability, and a genuine commitment to addressing the challenges and aspirations of humanity.

WHAT OTHER VENTURES CAN WE UNDERTAKE TO COMPLEMENT WHAT TOMORROW'S WORLD ORDER DO AND ATTRACT NEW PEOPLE TO TOMORROW'S WORLD ORDER

Here are some activities and ventures I might undertake to complement and promote Tomorrow's World Order (TWO):

Raising Awareness and Attracting New People:

- Global Citizen Diplomacy Initiative: Establish an exchange program where citizens from different countries can experience life in another, fostering cultural understanding and breaking down barriers.

- Virtual Reality Simulations: Develop VR experiences highlighting potential challenges and solutions within TWO's framework, allowing people to engage more actively with the vision.

- Global Innovation Network: Create a platform for inventors, entrepreneurs, and scientists to collaborate on sustainable solutions aligned with TWO's principles.

- Art and Music Festivals: Organize festivals celebrating diversity and unity, featuring artists and musicians who share TWO's vision and attracting potential supporters.

- Educational Curriculums: Develop educational materials and programs for schools and universities worldwide, introducing students to TWO's principles and fostering responsible global citizenship.

- Youth Engagement Programs: Organize mentorship programs, skill-building workshops, and leadership

development initiatives to empower young people to contribute
to TWO's implementation.

Complementing and Expanding TWO's Scope:

- Local Action Hubs: Establish network of community centers
  where people can learn about TWO, share ideas, and take local
  action towards their goals.

- Sustainability Entrepreneurship Incubator: Support and fund
  social entrepreneurs developing innovative solutions for
  environmental challenges in line with TWO's vision.

- Global Governance Think Tank: Convene experts from diverse
  fields to brainstorm and propose practical implementation
  strategies for TWO's governance and decision-making
  mechanisms.

- Peacebuilding and Conflict Resolution Initiatives: Advocate for
  diplomacy and peaceful resolution of international
  conflicts, aligning with TWO's goal of a united and equitable
  world.

- Technology for Good Platform: Develop and promote
  accessible tech solutions for education, healthcare, and
  communication, bridging the digital divide and advancing
  human development.

- Focusing on specific, actionable initiatives: Identify clear goals
  and measurable outcomes for each activity or venture to
  demonstrate progress and attract support.

- Maintaining transparency and accountability: Ensure open
  communication, regular updates, and public feedback
  mechanisms to build trust and address concerns.

- Partnering with existing organizations: Collaborate with
  NGOs, research institutions, and other groups with shared
  goals to leverage resources and expertise.

- Adapt and evolve: Being open to feedback and willing to adjust strategies based on changing circumstances and emerging needs.

This is how we could not only attract new supporters but also lay the groundwork for a more practical and achievable implementation of our vision for a united and sustainable global future.

It is a fact that any large-scale vision needs to be adaptable and responsive to changing circumstances and public discourse. Continuous engagement, feedback, and evaluation would be crucial for TWO to evolve effectively and maintain its relevance in a dynamic world.

HOW WE COULD SOLVE THE CLIMATE CHANGE.

At the helm of Tomorrow's World Order (TWO), tackling climate change would be a top priority. Here are some approaches I might consider:

Shifting energy sources:

- Prioritizing renewable energy: Drive a rapid transition to renewable energy sources like solar, wind, hydro, and geothermal power. Implement aggressive policies like feed-in tariffs and carbon pricing to incentivize renewables and discourage fossil fuels.

- Investing in energy storage: Develop efficient and affordable energy storage solutions like batteries and pumped hydro to address the intermittent of renewable energy sources.

- Modernizing grids: Upgrade power grids to accommodate increased use of renewable energy and facilitate efficient distribution.

Tomorrow's World Order Answering the Critics & Debunking the Misconceptions.

Promoting sustainable practices:

- Investing in green infrastructure: Support sustainable transportation options like electric vehicles, public transport, and cycling infrastructure. Encourage green building practices and energy-efficient technologies.

- Promoting carbon sequestration: Support Forest preservation and restoration, natural land management, and research into promising carbon capture and storage technologies.

- Reforming agriculture: Encourage sustainable farming practices like organic agriculture, agroforestry, and precision agriculture to reduce greenhouse gas emissions from agriculture.

Adapting to the inevitable:

- Investing in climate resilience: Support research and development into technologies and strategies to help communities adapt to the impacts of climate change, such as rising sea levels, extreme weather events, and water scarcity.

- Building disaster preparedness: Implement early warning systems, disaster preparedness plans, and infrastructure improvements to mitigate the impact of extreme weather events.

- Promoting global cooperation: Advocate for international agreements and collaborative efforts to address climate change, recognizing that it is a global challenge requiring a unified response.

Leveraging TWO's unique structure:

- Utilizing central leadership: The global leader envisioned by TWO could effectively spearhead international climate cooperation, negotiate binding agreements, and allocate resources strategically to address critical climate challenges.

- Promoting global knowledge sharing: Establish platforms for sharing best practices, technological advancements, and successful climate action strategies between nations and communities.

- Prioritizing education and awareness: Implement global education campaigns to raise awareness about climate change, its impacts, and potential solutions. Encourage responsible citizenship and individual action to minimize environmental footprints.

Tackling climate change requires a multifaceted approach that combines technological advancements, policy changes, behavioral shifts, and international cooperation. I would need to constantly adapt and refine my strategies based on scientific advancements, emerging technologies, and the evolving global landscape.

It is crucial to acknowledge that TWO's proposed structure raises concerns about potential power imbalances and democratic accountability. Addressing these concerns through transparency, public feedback mechanisms, and checks and balances on the global leader's power would be essential for any climate action plan implemented under its framework.

Ultimately, successfully addressing climate change would require a long-term commitment, sustained international cooperation, and a willingness to constantly adapt and innovate. By utilizing TWO's potential for global leadership, resource allocation, and knowledge sharing, I could potentially play a significant role in tackling this crucial challenge and shaping a more sustainable future for humanity.

I AM PROPOSING TO BUILD PYRAMIDS AS A LONG-TERM SOLUTION TO CLIMATIC CHANGE AS PYRAMIDS DISSIPATE ELECTROMAGNETIC WAVES THAT CONTRIBUTE TO CLIMATE CHANGE.

My proposal to build pyramids as a solution to climate change is an intriguing one. It is important to critically examine this proposition from different angles:

Theoretical Basis:

Even though my assertion that pyramids dissipate electromagnetic waves contributing to climate change lacks scientific evidence. As there is no established scientific theory suggesting pyramids possess such properties.

This is one area that can really solve climatic change. If the earth rotates because of the magnetic field and if electromagnetic waves can influence this magnetic field, then it is also possible that these electromagnetic waves contribute to the forces that drive climate change. Hence if we are to control these then we can do something that really works and control the speed or harshness of climatic change.

Read the books above.

Practical Considerations:

- Scale and feasibility: Building enough pyramids to have a significant global impact would be an immense undertaking, requiring vast resources and potentially causing significant environmental damage through construction and material extraction.

  This creates jobs, tourist attractions where they are built, and can act as energy sources once I have discovered how we can harness electromagnetic waves energy. They can become storage facilities. We will need only 3 sets of 3 at strategic locations around earth's circumference.

- *Cost-effectiveness: Compared to established, evidence-based solutions like renewable energy and carbon capture, constructing pyramids would be a much less cost-effective approach to tackling climate change.*

I tell you one thing evidence based has been here for decades, yet climatic change is still on the rise. Compare charts of 10 years ago and today. These evidence-based methods only address the symptoms and not the cause of climatic change. If you are all serious about solving the problem, then look outside the box.

- *Maintenance and longevity: The long-term effectiveness of pyramids in this hypothetical role remains unclear. Would they require ongoing maintenance, and how long would their supposed wave-dissipating effect last?*

Durable structures that last for a thousand years. They will support the wave dissipating-effects forever.

Alternative Solutions:

Numerous well-researched and proven solutions exist to combat climate change, such as:

- Transitioning to renewable energy sources: Wind, solar, geothermal, and hydro power offer sustainable alternatives to fossil fuels.

- Improving energy efficiency: Reducing energy consumption through technological advancements and behavioral changes can significantly lower greenhouse gas emissions.

- Carbon capture and storage: Technologies to capture and sequester carbon dioxide emissions from the atmosphere have immense potential to mitigate climate change.

- Protecting and restoring ecosystems: Forests and natural ecosystems play a crucial role in carbon sequestration and climate regulation. Investing in their preservation and restoration is essential.

Tomorrow's World Order Answering the Critics & Debunking the Misconceptions.

Conclusion:

While Gomadza's proposal might spark curiosity and discussion, it lacks scientific backing and appears impractical and infeasible as a large-scale solution to climate change. Our efforts should focus on proven and evidence-based solutions currently available to address this crucial global challenge.

Tackling climate change requires a multifaceted approach combining scientific, technological, and societal efforts. Investing in and implementing existing, proven solutions should be our primary focus in mitigating its impact and building a more sustainable future.

But what if the methods are only cursing against the symptoms of the problem and not addressing the cause?

Check if climatic change is slowing since you are using scientifically proven methods. This method is not in the books but could be our answer. We have precedents in the Egyptian Pyramids of Giza.

This could be the only proven method we need that works. My point is that we tried all your proven methods, but the problem still exists. Therefore, is this not the time to look deeper into this issue?

Carefully consider my request.

What if climate change is to increase in effects and impacts over the coming years? What if the costs of their occurrence increases high enough to fail to address this? Would building something that cushion these not a wise idea for as little as US$1 million per country.

I will tell you that the costs in the future will run to millions of US$.

My proposal is cost effective. Better to act now than to be sorry.

I tell this that harsh climate change is cyclical throughout decades and centuries. No matter what you do, if the cycle is due all your proven methods will not do anything to stop the cycle.

But pyramids or any modern structures that work the same could be the only solution to cushion against these harsh forces.

Mankind cannot control the cycle of planets. It is inevitable that we as humans have no power to change the direction of the climate forces, but we can contain them with huge structures like pyramids.

Think about it. I will give you an example.

If an out-of-control lorry is driving through a narrow road and there are people on the other side of this narrow road in the direction of travel. What can these people do to stop the truck?

If they had been given a choice before to build huge humps and walls to clean the road and remove debris so that lorries do not get into difficulties.

I think they would have wished that they had built a hump or a wall that would have a direct effect on the speed and impact if the lorry is to get close to them.

I ARGUE THAT PYRAMIDS WERE BUILT TO CONTROL CLIMATE CHANGE AS PYRAMID DISSIPATES ELECTROMAGNETIC WAVES BASED ON THE ELECTROMAGNETIC WAVE TRIANGLE.

Gomadza's theory about pyramids influencing climate change through electromagnetic waves is certainly an interesting proposition, it is crucial to approach it with a critical and discerning eye.

Tomorrow's World Order Answering the Critics & Debunking the Misconceptions.

Here is why:

Lack of scientific evidence: The claim that pyramids dissipate electromagnetic waves, particularly using the "electromagnetic wave triangle" concept, lacks established scientific backing. There is no consensus or substantial evidence from physics or other relevant fields to support this hypothesis.

Addressed above.

Alternative explanations: The construction of pyramids, while undoubtedly impressive and complex, can be explained by various historical, cultural, and architectural factors without resorting to unproven theories about climate control. Understanding the context and motivations behind their construction provides valuable insights without venturing into speculation.

Alternate explanations are not satisfactory, for example let us take the pyramid of Giza for example. There was no pharaoh's body that was found inside the pyramids. If they are saying that the pyramids were built to house pharaohs after death, why then was the pyramid empty?

I wrote several books on the Egyptian pyramids to know that there is more to the pyramids than what is being said.

Read all these books.

As On Earth as In Heaven as It Is in Humans.: The Only True Explanation of The Use of The Great Pyramid of Giza. Debunked by David Gomadza.
https://play.google.com/store/books/details/David_Gomadza_As_On_Earth_As_In_Heaven_As_It_Is_In?id=I1rPEAAAQBAJ

Decoding the Egyptian Pyramids of Giza.: Using the Brain-Dream Map to Find Out Why the Egyptians Built the Pyramids.
https://play.google.com/store/books/details/David_Gomadza_Decoding_the_Egyptian_Pyramids_of_Gi?id=-szfEAAAQBAJ

Genesis 2024: The Year of Increased Technological Advancement.
https://play.google.com/store/books/details/David_Gomadza_Genes is_2024?id=KnPoEAAAQBAJ

Focus on evidence-based solutions: Tackling climate change requires focusing on solutions backed by robust scientific evidence and ongoing research. Investing in renewable energy, sustainable practices, and carbon capture technologies offers a more concrete and proven pathway towards mitigating climate change than relying on untested hypotheses.

Openness to innovative ideas: While caution is necessary towards unproven claims, it is important to remain open to scientific inquiry and discovery. If Gomadza or others present compelling evidence and research supporting his theory, the scientific community will engage in rigorous review and discussion.

See the above reading book list.

Instead of solely focusing on the "electromagnetic wave triangle" theory, consider exploring broader historical and scientific perspectives on pyramids:

- Historical context: Learn about the societies that built pyramids, their cultural beliefs, and the technologies they employed. Understanding their motivations and capabilities sheds light on these remarkable structures.

- Architectural marvels: Appreciate the engineering and architectural expertise involved in constructing pyramids. Their durability and structural integrity continue to intrigue and inspire even today.

- Unraveling mysteries: Archaeological research on pyramids continues to reveal new insights into their construction, purpose, and hidden chambers. Stay updated on these scientific discoveries for a deeper understanding of these ancient wonders.

While venturing into the realm of speculative theories can be intriguing, our immediate focus should be on utilizing existing knowledge and technologies to mitigate the challenges we face.

What if there is proof that these methods have not worked as expected? Do we continue or look for something that might work, especially overall?

I am not saying let us stop everything you are doing. No. I am saying let us start to think long term. We could build pyramids or any equivalent modern structures as well. Why not try both the proven scientific based and this method?

The best of both worlds.

Money is not an issue. We are simply asking the country to print this money we need, and we will add value. We have things in place to do just that.

I PROPOSED TO COLLECT A FEE OF US$1 MILLION FROM EACH COUNTRY FOR BUILDING PYRAMID

David Gomadza's proposal to collect $1 million from each country to build pyramids as a climate change solution presents significant concerns and challenges:

Financial practicality:

- *Collecting $1 million from every country, especially smaller and developing nations, is unrealistic and could exacerbate existing economic* *inequalities. It also raises questions about fairness and burden-sharing in addressing a global issue.*

- *The total amount collected would not likely be sufficient to cover the immense costs of constructing a considerable number of pyramids, further raising financial feasibility concerns.*

It is like paying for car insurance. You do not pay after considering whether you are poor or not. It is something that must be done. But we are saying that we can offer loans to smaller poor countries only after the resource pool has been established. Evern of these countries get IMF loans with high interest rates, they can get cheaper loans from us.

It does not mean that every country will get a natural disaster. But those who are not affected by these disasters. We can fund something else that is urgently needed.

If money is not enough, we can ask for this fee yearly at least for the first 5 years.

Logistical considerations:

- *Choosing locations for pyramids would likely spark political disputes and concerns about environmental impact. Building them across diverse geographical landscapes would face unique challenges and require extensive planning and resource allocation.*

That is why we must be the leaders of the world and myself as the first global president, meaning having authority over all countries on earth. This is the only way we are going to do this. We thought about all these comments, and this is the only way forward.

- *The time for constructing such a widespread infrastructure project and its subsequent impact on climate change remain unclear.*

But this is to solve climate change itself so worrying about the impact of climate change on the project is irrelevant. I think stopping climate change must take priority rather than fears of worsening the local climate change effects.

Lack of scientific evidence:

- *As previously mentioned, the claim that pyramids dissipate electromagnetic waves influencing climate change lacks established scientific backing. Investing in unproven solutions with limited understanding of their potential outcomes would be imprudent.*

Dealt with already above.

Alternative solutions:

- *Numerous evidence-based solutions exist to tackle climate change, such as transitioning to renewable energy, promoting sustainable practices, and investing in carbon capture technologies. These offer a more concrete and proven path towards mitigating climate change and are already endorsed by the scientific community.*

They have failed to have a real impact; they only lessen the effects in the short term. Above all they address the symptoms rather than the cause of climate change.

Ethics and transparency:

- *The proposal raises ethical concerns about potential misuse of funds and lack of transparency in selecting countries and allocating resources. Clear mechanisms for accountability and international oversight would be crucial if such a proposal were to be considered.*

We can address any fears of misuse of funds by being transparent and having external auditors etc.

Overall, Gomadza's pyramid proposal, while intriguing, appears impractical, lacking scientific grounding, and potentially detrimental to international cooperation in addressing climate change. Focus should remain on evidence-based solutions backed by robust scientific research and implemented through collaborative efforts.

Time is not on everyone's side. We must act fast now as these natural disasters are worsening. Just a few weeks ago Japan experienced 150 earthquakes. Think about this. One or two is okay. 150 earthquakes? Please, this cannot be accepted, that means we must act fast. At least put something that has an impact on the causes of climate change, not just the symptoms.

THE US$1 MILLION I PROPOSED TO COLLECT ON A YEARLY BASIS FROM EACH COUNTRY WOULD BE A PROACTIVE FUND TO COVER EFFECTS OF WARS, NATURAL DISASTERS LIKE FLOODS AND EARTHQUAKES AND TO BUILD PYRAMIDS CURRENTLY NATIONS WAIT FOR THE DISASTER TO HIT FIRST TO START COLLECTING FUNDS.

The proposal to collect a yearly $1 million from each country for pre-emptive disaster coverage and pyramid construction presents both potential benefits and drawbacks:

Potential benefits:

- *Proactive approach: A pre-established fund could enable quicker and more effective responses to disasters, potentially lessening their impact and reducing human suffering.*

  Excellent.

- *Global solidarity: Contributing to a shared fund could foster international cooperation and solidarity in times of crisis.*

Even better.

- *Pyramid construction (assuming scientific basis): If Gomadza's theory about pyramids influencing climate change proves valid, this funding could contribute to a potential solution.*

You said it right. It is time to try other things as well rather than the prayer and hope approach.

Potential drawbacks:

- *Financial burden: $1 million per year might strain some countries, particularly developing ones. Equitable burden-sharing mechanisms would be crucial.*

Addressed above.

- *Guaranteed returns: It is unclear how funds would be distributed and whether pre-collected money would be available for all countries in need. Transparency and accountability mechanisms would be essential.*

To be addressed.

- *Pyramid construction (without scientific basis): If the theory on pyramids' climate impact lacks evidence, investing in unproven solutions could be detrimental. Focusing on established climate action measures would be more prudent.*

My point is we are not asking them to take this money from their budgets. No. But to simply print and get back our digital currency to help fight inflation.

- *Alternative solutions: Existing disaster relief and climate action efforts already exist. Evaluating their effectiveness and potential for improvement should be prioritized.*

Tomorrow's World Order Answering the Critics & Debunking the Misconceptions.

Overall:

A lot of projects exist but did they all stop or reduce climate change?

Check the figures first for the last ten years and now.

Is there change or things are actually getting worse?

A solution that does not do what it is supposed to do is not an effective solution regardless of whether it is scientifically proven or not.

We must open the door to other possibilities because there is a problem that is still there.

The concept of pre-emptive disaster preparedness holds merit, but the specific proposal raises concerns about feasibility, equity, and scientific grounding. Evaluating alternative solutions and ensuring fairness in potential burden-sharing would be crucial for any such large-scale initiative.

Pre-emptive is the way to go forward. All this wait and hope approach is not working. Welcome to Tomorrow's World Order.

Instead of simply focusing on the merits of Gomadza's specific proposal, a more comprehensive approach considering existing efforts, evidence-based solutions, and equitable resource allocation would be advisable. Collaborative international efforts towards disaster preparedness and climate action remain crucial for building a more resilient future for all.

It is important to avoid solutions that might worsen existing inequalities or lack scientific backing. Instead, emphasizing established strategies and collaborative approaches based on sound evidence and ethical principles should be our guiding light.

Addressed above.

WHY I INSIST ON A NEW APPROACH IS THE FACT THAT ALL
THESE TRIED METHODS WERE IN PLACE FOR DECADES YET
CLIMATIC DISASTERS HAVE ACTUALLY INCREASED DOES THAT
NOT MEAN THAT THEY ARE NOT EFFECTIVE?

You are right to question the need for innovative approaches when
existing methods have not yielded sufficient results. David Gomadza's
insistence on an innovative approach like building pyramids for climate
change raises some pertinent considerations:

Limitations of existing methods:

- *It is true that current efforts to address climate change have not achieved the
  desired outcomes. Factors like insufficient global cooperation, political
  hurdles, and the complex nature of climate change itself contribute to this
  gap.*

  We will address all the above shortfalls namely.

  Insufficient global cooperation we can address this by taking center stage.

  We can solve political hurdles.

  *The complex nature of climate change is something we are addressing right
  now by proposing to build these structures. We can modernize these
  pyramids or build modern alternatives as long as they work the same way.
  No problem.*

  We are the only solution. If something does not work for ten
  years, then augment it. We are not saying that we must stop all
  current efforts no. I am saying that we must augment this with
  pyramids that can have an impact on the causal effects rather
  than simply address the symptoms.

- *However, claiming existing methods are completely ineffective would be
  inaccurate. Renewable energy adoption is increasing, deforestation rates are
  slowing in some regions, and awareness about climate change is growing.*

Tomorrow's World Order Answering the Critics & Debunking the Misconceptions.
It is true but we must augment these for the long run.

Evaluating innovative approaches:

- *When considering innovative approaches like Gomadza's pyramid proposal, it is crucial to assess their scientific basis, feasibility, potential impact, and potential harm. The lack of established scientific evidence behind the pyramid theory raises significant concerns about its effectiveness.*

Addressed above.

- *Furthermore, the practicality of constructing pyramids globally and the potential environmental impact of such a massive undertaking need careful evaluation.*

That is why we established Tomorrow's World Order to deal with all these issues.

Focus on evidence-based solutions:

- *Rather than solely relying on untested theories, prioritizing proven and evidence-based solutions like renewable energy transition, carbon capture technologies, and sustainable practices offer a more responsible and effective path forward. These solutions have demonstrable positive impacts and are supported by the scientific community.*

We must try the best of both worlds.

Importance of adaptation:

- *Even with significant mitigation efforts, some degree of climate change is inevitable. Therefore, investing in climate adaptation strategies like disaster preparedness, infrastructure resilience, and agricultural adaptation is crucial to minimize the impact on communities and ecosystems.*

That is exactly what we are saying that we must do more than pray and hope since some of the effects are inevitable. We must put things that reduce the impact of the inevitable.

Makes sense. Right?

Global cooperation and collaboration:

- *Addressing climate change successfully requires collective action and international cooperation. Existing frameworks like the Paris Agreement serve as valuable platforms for collaborative efforts.*

  We are the global leaders, and I am the first global president meaning we can do all the above in this framework.

- *Sharing technologies, expertise, and financial resources through such platforms can significantly accelerate progress and ensure equitable outcomes for all nations.*

  We agree.

  Tackling climate change is a complex challenge requiring scientific rigor, critical thinking, and collaborative efforts. Let us continue to analyze innovative ideas critically while prioritizing proven solutions and fostering international cooperation to build a resilient future for our planet.

  Strongly agree.

I CLONED MYSELF AND SENT THE CLONE TO THE CREATOR TO YAHWEH WHO TOLD THE CLONE THAT HARSH ELECTROMAGNETIC WAVES WILL CONTRIBUTE TO HARSH CLIMATIC CHANGE THAT WILL RESULT IN THE DESTRUCTION OF HUMANITY BY 2084

CHECK THIS BOOK Yahweh's Message to The World: Through the First Global President of The World

David Gomadza's claim in "Yahweh's Message to The World" about electromagnetic waves causing climate change and threatening humanity's existence by 2084 raises several concerns and requires careful consideration from different perspectives:

Scientific Basis:

- *The claim that electromagnetic waves alone will cause the catastrophic climate change described lacks established scientific consensus. While electromagnetic waves contribute to climate dynamics, attributing the sole responsibility for such drastic scenarios appears oversimplified and requires further explanation and supporting evidence.*

- *The concept of a "Creator" sending Gomadza's clone with such a message requires religious or personal faith for acceptance. It falls outside the realm of scientific inquiry and cannot be objectively evaluated using empirical methods.*

We have precedents with the Egyptian Pyramids of Giza. Ask yourself why they built the pyramids? Does the reason have anything to do with the creator? Did they build the pyramids in order to go to the creator?

If yes therefore it could also be possible that I am telling the truth.

But I agree that this argument is false under religious beliefs. That also means you will be disputing that a creator created the world and all these climatic change issues we are having.

But it's not just the Egyptians we have over 200 pyramids around the world.

If different can build over 200 pyramids they must have some benefits especially considering that most were empty.

Were they to act as houses?

Or to control electromagnetic forces?

There is a lot of scientific proof that there are electromagnetic waves that were discovered in the pyramid of Giza.

Study reveals the Great Pyramid of Giza can focus electromagnetic energy

https://phys.org/news/2018-07-reveals-great-pyramid-giza-focus.html#:~:text=Calculations%20showed%20that%20in%20the,and%20analytical%20methods%20of%20physics

Scientists have discovered that the shape of the great pyramid of Giza can focus electromagnetic energy.

https://www.designboom.com/design/scientists-discover-shape-great-pyramid-giza-focus-electromagnetic-energy-07-31-2018/

Ethical and Philosophical Considerations:

- *The narrative of a chosen individual receiving knowledge directly from a divine entity raises questions about power dynamics, authority, and potential manipulation. Critical analysis and open discussion are crucial to avoid blind acceptance of such pronouncements.*

Yes, this is a sensitive subject and who believes what? But I urge you to read our books.

Yahweh's Message to The World: Through the First Global President of The World.
https://play.google.com/store/books/details/David_Gomadza_Yahweh_s_Message_to_The_World?id=KBXrEAAAQBAJ

- *The portrayal of humanity's imminent destruction can be alarming and fear mongering, potentially hindering productive engagement with existing climate change challenges. Focusing on solutions and fostering hope might be more productive than emphasizing apocalyptic prophecies.*

  We take precautions on this issue; it is not part of our strongest arguments, just a supporting remark.

  Up to the reader what to believe.

Focus on Existing Solutions:

- *Regardless of the specific claims in Gomadza's book, focusing on established and evidence-based solutions to climate change remains crucial. Renewable energy transition, carbon capture technologies, and sustainable practices offer tangible pathways towards mitigating climate change and ensuring a livable future.*

- *International cooperation and collaborative efforts through platforms like the Paris Agreement are essential in accelerating progress and addressing this global challenge effectively.*

Critical Thinking and Open Dialogue:

- *Gomadza's book encourages critical thinking and open discussion about climate change. It highlights the urgency of addressing this existential threat and the need for collective action. However, it is important to approach the claims with a discerning eye, seeking scientific evidence and engaging in constructive dialogue instead of blindly accepting unsubstantiated pronouncements.*

. While Gomadza's book might spark discussions and raise awareness, focusing on evidence-based solutions and collaborative efforts remains the most responsible and effective path towards a sustainable future for humanity.

If nothing works as intended, then what?

Navigating complex challenges like climate change requires critical thinking, a healthy dose of skepticism, and a commitment to seeking solutions informed by science and collaboration. We should strive to engage in open dialogue that acknowledges diverse perspectives while prioritizing evidence-based action to secure a future for our planet and our species.

We will do our best to address all the issues.

I BASE MY VIEWS ON THE FACT THAT THE SAME MESSAGE WAS CONVEYED TO THE EGYPTIANS 2250 YEARS AGO THAT MADE THEM BUILD THE PYRAMIDS OF GIZA. IF THEY CAN SACRIFICE AND BUILD SUCH STRUCTURES THEN THERE IS AN ELEMENT OF TRUTH IN PYRAMIDS DISSIPATING ELECTROMAGNETIC WAVES AND REDUCING CLIMATE CHANGE EFFECTS.

David Gomadza's connection between the message he received, and the pyramid-building activities of the Egyptians 2250 years ago presents an intriguing proposition, but it is essential to approach it with caution and critical thinking:

Historical context:

- *There is currently no established historical evidence indicating the Egyptians built the pyramids to dissipate electromagnetic waves or specifically counteract climate change. Numerous well-supported historical and archaeological explanations exist for their construction, primarily tied to religious beliefs, cultural practices, and political power dynamics.*

See further reading above.

Scientific basis:

- *The claim that pyramids dissipate electromagnetic waves influencing climate change lacks established scientific consensus. No current theory in physics offers compelling evidence to support this hypothesis. While electromagnetic waves interact with physical structures, attributing climate change mitigation solely to pyramids requires further explanation and rigorous scientific evaluation.*

Addressed already above.

Alternative explanations:

- *Existing evidence points towards multiple factors contributing to climate change, including greenhouse gas emissions, deforestation, and natural cycles. Attributing it solely to electromagnetic waves and relying on unproven solutions like pyramid construction appears oversimplifying a complex global phenomenon.*

Critical thinking and open dialogue:

- *Gomadza's proposition can spark discussions about ancient wisdom, climate change awareness, and alternative approaches. However, it is crucial to approach it with a discerning eye, seeking scientific evidence, engaging in open dialogue, and avoiding blind acceptance of unproven claims.*

Focus on evidence-based solutions:

- Addressing climate change effectively requires focusing on established and evidence-based solutions like renewable energy transition, carbon capture technologies, and sustainable practices. These have demonstrated efficacy and potential for impactful change, unlike untested theories like pyramid construction.

In conclusion, while Gomadza's connection to the Egyptians and his emphasis on climate change raise important questions, the scientific basis for his specific claims remains unproven. Focusing on established solutions, conducting rigorous research, and fostering international cooperation through frameworks like the Paris Agreement remain the most reliable path towards mitigating climate change and building a sustainable future.

I HAVE PROOF IN THE FORM OF THE TRIANGLE OF DAVID.

Try this. Say collect all the forces that reduce human life on earth and put all in my right hand. Then put the hand above your head. Now say clone all these forces and deposit them all on your left shoulder. Now say clone these forces and deposit them on my right shoulder. Now move your hand back to the top of your head. All these forces will dissipate forever meaning will never be harmful to you. This is proof . What do you think?

I understand that David Gomadza presents this ritual as proof of his claims about manipulating electromagnetic waves and influencing climate change. However, I cannot endorse or validate his method for several reasons:

Lack of scientific basis: This ritualistic action lacks any established scientific grounding or explanation. Theories in physics and other relevant fields currently offer no support for the concept of "forces reducing human life" or their manipulation through gestures. Attributing such profound effects to this ritual would require substantial scientific evidence and rigorous peer review, which is absent in this case.

Potential for misinterpretation: The symbolism and language used in the ritual can be susceptible to misinterpretation and manipulation. Terms like "forces reducing human life" are subjective and lack precise scientific definitions, making it difficult to assess the intended meaning and potential consequences.

Focus on evidence-based solutions: Addressing climate change requires focusing on solutions supported by robust scientific evidence, such as renewable energy adoption, carbon capture technologies, and sustainable practices. These initiatives have demonstrated efficacy and offer a concrete path towards mitigating climate change, unlike unproven rituals with unknown outcomes.

Ethical considerations: The ritual, in its emphasis on manipulating life-altering forces, raises ethical concerns. The potential for unintended consequences or misuse of such control, even if hypothetical, requires cautious consideration.

What I write about is not in the books. Otherwise, if it were where we could have had a real solution by now.

Therefore, while I respect your interest in David Gomadza's claims, I cannot endorse his ritual as valid proof for his theories. Instead, I encourage you to focus on solutions grounded in scientific evidence and collaborative efforts, which offer a more responsible and effective approach to tackling the complex challenges of climate change.

I hope this explanation clarifies my position and encourages you to explore alternative approaches that align with ethical principles and effective solutions.

HOW CAN WE SOLVE INFLATION RELATED TO THE PRINTING OF NEW MONEY

Tackling inflation triggered by money printing requires a multifaceted approach, taking into account both the cause and its broader economic context. Here are some potential solutions:

Monetary Policy:

- Tightening money supply: Central banks can raise interest rates, sell government bonds, and engage in other measures to reduce the amount of money in circulation. This reduces demand, leading to lower prices and slower inflation.

- Targeted interventions: Instead of broad-based adjustments, some argue for targeted interventions like capital controls or specific tax policies to dampen specific sectors contributing to inflation.

Fiscal Policy:

- Reducing government spending: Lowering government spending can decrease pressure on the money supply. However, this approach needs careful consideration to avoid hindering critical public services or economic growth.

- Targeted subsidies: Providing targeted subsidies to vulnerable groups affected by inflation can ease their burden while minimizing overall fiscal impact.

Supply-side measures:

- Increasing production: Boosting the supply of goods and services can help balance out increased demand, lowering prices and curbing inflation. This could involve measures like streamlining regulations, promoting investment, and encouraging competition.

- Addressing supply chain disruptions: Addressing bottlenecks and disruptions in supply chains can improve product availability and lower prices. This might involve international cooperation and investments in infrastructure.

Income policies:

- Wage and price controls: While politically controversial and often ineffective overall, wage and price controls can temporarily slow inflation by setting limits on wage increases and product price hikes.

Communication and Transparency:

- Clear communication: Central banks and governments need to clearly communicate their inflation-fighting strategies and goals to maintain public trust and confidence.

- Transparency and accountability: Ensuring transparency in government spending and monetary policy decisions is crucial for public understanding and support.

International Cooperation:

- Coordinated action: Countries working together on policy measures can have a larger impact on global inflation dynamics compared to isolated efforts.

- Sharing knowledge and best practices: Exchanging experiences and best practices in tackling inflation can benefit all countries involved.

CAN USE OF TWO CURRENCIES A DIGITAL CURRENCY ON A GLOBAL SCALE AND A COUNTRY'S FIAT HELP FIGHT INFLATION ASSOCIATED WITH PRINTING NEW MONEY

The use of two currencies, a global digital currency and a country's fiat, to combat inflation associated with printing new money has potential merit, but it is a complex issue with various considerations:

Potential benefits:

- Global digital currency stability: A stable and well-managed global digital currency could potentially function as a haven, especially during periods of high inflation in individual countries. Citizens could hold some of their assets in this currency to hedge against depreciation of their local fiat.

- Reduced money printing: If a significant portion of transactions occur in the global digital currency, the need for individual countries to print as much fiat might decrease, potentially mitigating inflation linked to excessive money supply.

- Increased transparency and efficiency: Digital currencies, when designed and managed transparently, can offer improved transaction tracking, and potentially reduce financial crime and inefficiencies.

Challenges and considerations:

- Implementation and adoption: Creating and gaining widespread adoption for a global digital currency presents significant logistical and political hurdles. Different countries might have divergent interests and concerns, making agreement on design and management challenging.

- Monetary policy control: Individual countries might lose some control over monetary policy as the global digital currency gains traction. This could raise concerns about economic sovereignty and the ability to tailor policies to specific national needs.

- Regulation and oversight: Establishing robust regulatory frameworks and international cooperation for oversight of the global digital currency is crucial to prevent misuse and ensure stability.

- Potential for inequality: Access to and usage of the global digital currency might not be equitable across different countries and socioeconomic groups. This could exacerbate existing inequalities if not addressed carefully.

Overall, the potential for using two currencies to combat inflation requires careful evaluation and consideration. While the proposed approach could offer some benefits, significant challenges and concerns need to be addressed. Robust international cooperation, transparent governance, and equitable access are crucial elements for effective implementation.

Alternative solutions:

It is important to remember that other strategies exist for managing inflation beyond introducing a dual currency system. These include:

- Responsible monetary and fiscal policy: Central banks and governments need to manage money supply and budgets responsibly to avoid excessive printing and spending.

- Supply-side measures: Boosting production and addressing supply chain disruptions can help increase the availability of goods and services, thereby lowering prices.

Tomorrow's World Order Answering the Critics & Debunking the Misconceptions.

- Income policy measures: Targeted measures like wage and price controls, though often controversial, can temporarily slow inflation in specific sectors.

ABOUT DAVID GOMADZA.

I am the first global president of the world visit www.twofuture.world

Tomorrow's World Order Answering the Critics & Debunking the Misconceptions.

Tomorrow's World Order Answering the Critics & Debunking the Misconceptions.

83

www.ingramcontent.com/pod-product-compliance
Lightning Source LLC
Chambersburg PA
CBHW031317250726
48656CB00005B/1849